FRAGILE ACTS

Fragile Acts

ALLAN PETERSON

McSWEENEY'S
POETRY SERIES

M^CSWEENEY'S
SAN FRANCISCO

www.mcsweeneys.net

Cover art by Jacob Magraw-Mickelson
Calligraphy on title page by Frances Dunham

The McSweeney's Poetry Series is edited by
Dominic Luxford and Jesse Nathan.

This book was typeset in Fournier.

ISBN: 978-1-936365-80-7

Printed in Michigan by Thomson-Shore

811
PETERSON,
A.

Contents

FRAGILE ACTS

THE TOTALITY OF FACTS

The laughing gull that flew behind the fencepost
and never came out was the beginning
and then a hand smaller than my hand covered Wisconsin
with a gesture for explanation.
In the afternoon there are pauses between the words
through which commas can grow like daisy fleabane.
A fish with an osprey in its back emerges from the Sound
and nothing can be learned by more analysis.
The book of her hair opens to its binding and I leaf through
the glorious pages of appreciation and that's not all.
We could not have turned fast enough to catch
light and leftovers from so much of what happened:
the swift figures behind you like a planet's dark
companion, ships entering and leaving the hall closet
the real and imagined between which is no difference.

The Influence of Dress on Architecture

In the long and poignant relationship with matter,
to be built is to be born.
The young fern curled is like your hand
sleeping on the chair in green silk under the curtain wall,
able with fingers to elaborate the ragged shadows.
It has never made sense that we celebrate the days
since the death of someone as if a joy,
instead of the height of life, June 2, when the schefflera
seemed angels dancing up the walls, October 5,
when seeing your face, theirs broke out in water,
circles rippling from their mouths outward.
How it was to be inside the ornament built by feeling,
the spoon-sized light among scrolls and volutes,
the wearing of a building like a thinkable skin.
To have been animate like a sequined component of blood,
body walls basic as personal astrologers to the queen
in which gravity is evident, then parting to columns,
to fingers, to legs, to the pleated see-through sheath
with dependable results.
The cornice, as Ruskin says,
as a hand opened to carry something above its head,
a fern, a course of tile, a scarf set aside for pleasure.

Innocence or Proof

Fast clouds are pelicans the others merely gas and obscurantists.

Water's face is laughing on the ceiling on the porch next door.

Blue jays visit the dog chow because they are big enough then drink

and the reflecting face changes to glitter stew or the cat returns

and water gets the joke how some beautiful moon over the ocean

may turn out to be plastic dinnerware as those photos of flying

saucers were pan lids and lamp shades. What use is innocence or proof.

What if they just told us blackbirds are only sucking color from things

around them maybe a mixed inheritance of coal and impressionism

or how you can sweat like crazy and play electric bass and not be electrocuted

unless you touch two E strings at once he said inferring from the stories

of birds fried on the powerlines once their tails hit the one behind.

As I Understand It

The dots in the star charts are the same size
as the roaches leave
on the mouse pad and the drawings
and dreams are coming so fast they're numbered
like days or the nonstellar objects
in the NGC
And since the sky starts right outside my fingers
and extends inconceivably far—
way past QSO 0957 and 561 the double quasar
acting as a gravitational lens
it fails as a simplifying concept since it holds everything
even heaven
nothing more than a shepherd's idea of politics
and something unreachable
you promise to the kids for their own good
gold everywhere a floating throne
As I understand it
the people with wings on their backs like us
flew out from our fingers
that clench and lax all night that touch our hazardous
flocks of bones and quasars at once

EIGHT PRESIDENTS

October five. Seven years older in dog years and then your November
the day record snowfalls hit Randolph New Hampshire in forty-three
and I am thinking of something intimate and impossible to waste:
Brazil's undiscovered caverns of amethyst   endless smooth oval stones
along Washington's moody Pacific chewing a continent. But I am wrong.
We pass St. Michael's the cemetery that asks the public to mow and weed it
and perhaps draw larger conclusions about the already wasted and tidy up names
frayed at the edges by the ions that bind   by age the chemical salt of time
that jostles stones over at their bases to remind us or alter their sentiments.
We read and read and each time nothing new has come up on their markers.
At home we hear the fishermen bring up their nets smack water to scare them.
By now the flounder's secret pocket where its heart and everything separate
from meat and bone is cleaned and empty as a silk purse not a nickel left
down in the freezer. Nothing really shines but this: I have loved you
eight presidents. Forty years. Five point seven in dog.

HUNGER FOR SUBSTANCES

I know you have heard of them, the finches
adapted to diet
whose beaks accommodate the shapes of hunger,
moon snails
which are said to be shark's eyes lost or cast off,
overgrown or cloudy
from disuse, while somewhere one-eyes cruise
above a reef.
And the paradox of the so-called living rock
out of which Petra
and Rushmore carved without a woman, amazing
but great waste.
And you have seen the young buy silver chains
against losing
a wallet, really just metals in place of plumage,
and a hunger
for substances strong as the moon that can't
take its eye off us.

No Spare Time

As if a commodity, as if someone managed well enough
there might be some left over
to be squandered or put by, a demonstration of the brain
people say you use only one-tenth of,
the rest nothing but a home for illusions of spirit, taxation,
a man on the moon.

No, it is like the air, this tercet of January, the new year filling
every calendar at once
as soon as the young numbers stand up.
The underbird is gull white so it can't be seen against the sky,
and grey above so it can't likewise be lunch meat
against the sea like last week, but new.

It has taken years to dismantle the brain, cell by cell,
to find the place of the origin of sleep, the suprachiasmatic nucleus,
a little bouquet in the hippocampus.
Now we can look for the center of the ability to draw the U.S.
from memory. We can,
uttering the charmed name of Wilder Penfield, touch wires to a gyrus,
find the remains of primitive birds
in the asphalt of a parking lot, see what monster under the bed
is re-elected to consciousness, which part stimulated

speaks heresy.

In one of the anomalies of vision, I stare at the wharf pilings

till they turn to flashlights,

white shafts shooting up from the gull perches.

The idea fills the moment like someone in 1610 receiving a copy

of Galileo's Starry Messenger,

Sidereus Nuncius, with pictures of the moon in raking light.

Falling Behind

The explosion was pure bad taste,
though its mum above the desert added another regretful abstract
on beauty to the files.
Cross-referenced under hideous/extreme, it was another hybrid
of insecurity's green thumb.
We all do this out of amazement and lifelong talking to the air.
Not prayer, but for a moment the other
living inside us is given external life
to file the motions and briefs of amended sorrows.

I will never catch up is one. This morning I saw a new spider
in the ilex, two stripes vermilion,
but I will not find it in the always deficient guidebook
or find out why it never sticks to its own web.
Ollie appeared to be resting in her death drawer, resting and listening
to the talk and singing in her gold sequins
each a silent owl's eye, an elaborate example of exquisite limitations.
No Tuesdays. No blooms. No *Fodor's* on tomorrow.
No thinking back to only a stunning moment ago.

EPISTEMOLOGY FOLLOWS

The ocean seems endless when two dolphins divide it.
Epistemology follows. We know they have bones
below their smiles because two lost vertebrae sail
in our standing glass cabinet. Phylogeny follows.
The linked oceans are peptides cleaved by those dorsals
so the gene of understanding can be inserted by thought.
Years ago trains threw oars of light from their windows.
In the endless black you could see them rowing through Kansas
while someone's lost rings were being taken up inside the bark
of a honey locust that sparkled in the leaves each spring.
Nostalgia is another way of knowing. Now the first
cannot happen. We have no dark places anymore. Even in Kansas
we can see the small towns from satellites. See license plates.
And the second cannot happen. We don't marry long enough
to have trees capable of swallowing the past though we lose everything.
We look away   learn nothing   let the black ocean close over us
again as if nothing knowable ever happened that we could swim to
dig up or learn from. No life rafts, no Occam's razor.

SURVIVAL

One of the times you are almost fatally interested in your body.
Blackout from too much of something. Your eyes trying to fly.
Their lids fluttered almost too tired or the line was busy
or the call cannot be completed as dialed though we never dial
anymore we touch. A few whispered muscles losing control
the letters on each button spelling help on the way.
Overhead leaves are moving clouds as fingers do beads
on a straight pool counter-wire in smoky surroundings.
For those who believe it this episode might fool the soul
into leaving early slipping out between eyelids like jump ropes
the feeling of entering the Funhouse the Tunnel of Love banging
through the interior set of double doors into the populated dark.
Entropy: energy lost. Disorganization that occupies the night
down to the bubbles in a sponge. A few other things
have changed: some of the same wars still on
and we're losing them all. That's about it for survival.
In cartoons "knocked out" has little stars orbiting a head.
It means some knowledge is interior and brings its own light
from the Egocentric System though you may need a bump on the head
to remember or hands from behind over your eyes that say *guess*
why the universe is leaving why geography is floating on batter
and all our historical bodies give off endless white bones instead of light.

What the Usual Has Become

For the misery of the body
there are houses, the same for delight.
The ghosts of both are holding our attention
and not with gloomy intonations of the common ruin,
the end of calamities and back spasms
but so subtle it seems nothing is missing but a few frogs
from our yard to California. By the time we notice
they are half dead of what the usual has become.

It is a sad thing
to see a cow falter with palsy, sheep from scours,
cousin Earl stymied by his name and aunt Belle feeding him.
Now after amphibians comes word our seahorses
are declining worldwide. They mention it tenderly
—our seahorses—delicate and fragile as if knowing
the males brood offspring the ocean would be a shrine
seahorse a savior and we would rush
to restore the toxic waters.

For the mystery of the body
there is relentless arrogance and poor understanding.
No wonder nothing comes to us
but what's afraid to be eaten if it refuses.

If we were to graph trends, the declining corkscrew of belief
like the Devil's dick would diminish to wood smoke,
the favorite telephone of bloodthirsty deities
who can't tell a lamb from a forest fire.

LONG DISTANCE

Astronauts say their dreams are like earth dreams
but the people are floating.
Last night when Frances answered her dream phone
I was down under the pastry layers
of sheets and blue throw. Later she asked did I hear it.
No, I had been orbiting myself,
misreading a box in Carol's kitchen "cloudless" for cordless.
At night when stars fall on Alabama
water goes granular and steps back, dreams improve us
with their thick pastels, revisits in tints.
Maybe the astronauts called from their cloudless telephones
with news from Long Distance:
Romans invaded Arabia Felix, Columbus discovered Ohio.

MOONBATHING

Those speaking Latin are the doctors and gardeners.
Cleyera Japonica. Dementia Praecox.
Before I was born a grandfather added himself
to the rafters, tongue a black tulip.
Something was unbearable, dementia like a grinning weed,
letters from Denmark, insects
infesting the compass rose.

Sunsleeping.

Your ivy dies and you put at risk the evermore,
each flower speaking with a doctor's voice
its double names: urgency and dread.
If you listened you could hardly move.
The gravity of the body
is a weight that extinguishes itself. I towel off the light,
the iris is apparently screaming
but so high we miss the blame.

Subdivisions within the Idea of Place

Morning's celebrity, the spatula, sharpens on the grill
a stage of spotlight egg shells broken near the whet.
Plant leaves under my window make fake eyes of moisture
hiding my face in each one among the only-known-as-weeds.
Poetry's a way of knowing how gods arise from a scramble
of feedback loops, the dying and reviving deities we want
to be like. A gold next-door dog, *Déjà vu*, turns black
against the light like silver on paper and the lattice
Alan nailed to his boathouse becomes transparent
when the sun goes down behind it in plain words.
Embellishment is love. Elaboration is a lover's response
to the numinous. Decoration is importance demonstrated
by its flourishes. Symmetries gilded and flattered with acanthus.
Beauty, inflorescence, light bulbs wrapped in tinfoil.

Seeing It Coming

A blast of colored electrons coming from the screen
we gave up for silence
would have summarized the cold front.
The National Seashore's Visitor's Center has taken to putting
silhouette hawks
on its windows to keep songbirds from crashing the glass,
white cutouts.
We fear hearing the same at home, the occasional but firm
pillowed thuds,
the sound inside of which is the cracked sternum
the broken neck
or the dazed flicker imagining a tree struck back.

When Aretha sings *another link in the chain*,
I am thinking carbon,
polysaccharides strung like lights and vertebrae,
then the splashed flag
on the glass, birds without bladders. This morning
the yard is begging,
young birds pleading, first time flyers,
the closer the mother the more urgent.
Inside the voice is emergency
so explicit there are harps
and sirens,

the parents so acute they see distant insects. We've watched

a thrasher fly straight

from a pine top to pick a moth no bigger than a syrinx.

Today, we found one

under the window, still with a berry in it its mouth,

ants discussing its eyes.

MEDUSAS

Smoke rising up curls down the same shapes

as ink through water

placed lightly with a dropper

medusas fall like petticoats spread wide

and fall within falling

There are things beyond the senses

but we are not built for them

We do not know their number or the number

we contain or where our edges are

We infer them from the apparently miraculous

As ink forms a Man O' War

in the drinking glass Ophelia floats neatly

face up eyes open

under the river bridge   dress spread like a farthingale

staring elsewhere one hand open

one curled tightly on what we cannot see

In the society of glass, one shatters for the least mistake.
Delicate is dangerous, the risks preceded by cautions.
In the fragile acts of memory even a goblet is poignant,
it shudders, it sings one wet finger on the rim.

In the silence of stone is the discernible eloquence of fire.
Redundance is characteristic of the ancient earth opening the hours,
geodes, little earths, riches instilled in the glassy magmas.

Transparent voices enter even the radios of Hotchkiss, Colorado.
Poignancy and singing load the air composed of nothing
but recollection floating above us into the atmosphere.

What was it like ask the songs, that world remembered
with all of history see-through and all of the present vitrines,
liquid, life like rose windows, glinting with what if's, as if's,
precious, fragile, next to nothing.

It was like a laser pointed at a shattered vase in Corning
and having a portion of the fractured beams theoretically fall
on the faces of apparently floating kings in Westminster,

like Ruskin in Switzerland drawing in a few inches of charcoal
what he said was the edge of a mile of Matterhorn.

It was like the geese on pink legs herded by Harry McCue
with the beam of a flashlight from pasture to the barn
while standing on his porch sheep-dogging their bodies.

It was like drawing at the same time water on the yard
as if Western New York had been cut loose from limestone.

It was a collection of collections, accrual,
like everywhichway signposts at crossroads.

It was how ribs for the barn roof were a boat overturned.
It was wearing expectations like a luminous string of perils.

It was more, it was greater than

>

It was like opening *Webster's* to "emptiness," *void*,
the invisible axis around which a rose opens,
the disappearance inside the "o" of the ring binder,
a hole leading to nothing but another like itself
and a blank page awaiting explanation.

It was the heron that stood before me
like something from a manuscript, a guide,
and when it spoke the ancient opened, and I opened
another page to "adze," the instrument restoring speech
to the dead in the hands of Anubis.

>

It was like sometimes the overwhelming seemed enough,
singing when sung to, writing to when written,
coming early, staying late.

>

It was like the dogs were already howling,
the moon just happened to be there.

>

It was like all expectation, never starting from the dead
and working backwards to the passion of its advocates,
but starting from the baby, reliving the rest of us.

It was like we were trying to look famous once or twice,
forgetting that Pavlov learned to drool with his dogs.

It was a long way from equilibrium

>

It was velocity
where victims on impact left their shoes,
bodies turned rubber in an instant,
and pointed questions pierced their hearts.

It was trouble and difficulty even if we needed
trouble and difficulty, like someone nearby
conversing quietly with downfall, waking from a dream
of three horses stepping from their skins,
to find they had slipped from their covers to the floor.

It was erasable footsteps on water.

It was like give us this day a silver Mercedes.

It was like finding the lost hikers near the canyon floor.

It was like the eclipse assisted Columbus.

>

It was like speech was the energy that organized the system
when we said some things burn down while others burn up,
sometimes the same things.

Running Out

So what is it straight from the shoulder
or the heart you want to hear.
Hooting from the hip or the disappearing
vision from eyes behind me
or how much diminishment it takes
before we notice the most meaningful instances:
water shuddering in one place,
asleep in another.

To have seasons in the South,
mothers spray snow in the window corners,
spear paper cups like flowers
on yuccas and the Spanish bayonets.

So we cannot begin at the beginning,
being in the middle already.
Even in sequence, parse is only one page
from the paramecia we would interrogate
with light and knives.
The crown of thorns,
a symbolic opportunist in any field,
erodes the brains,
the glitter that is no longer with us, but stands

for everyone in a hideous way,
uncaring while interested, our wills an edifice of it
as though thousands were near as the birdbath.

So there will be grass, and then a buffalo
from a camera affixed to a Land Rover at Umfolozi.
There will be the shy way
the sundew hides its stems in our own yard, news
from the western fires on email,
blazing spiders housekeeping in the heart.

MORE

We want more, but more is an emergent property.
It comes for you out of the same constituents
as when you were nothing but them yourself,
from the unspoken, the far place
nickels disappeared with their buffalos.
Most of us never believed the ordinary
was that miraculous, the complex reducible
completely to a few brash headlines.
Look at the inquisitive miles fingers have put on pianos,
knocking softly though nothing opened.
Perhaps the pretty demons inside failed to hear
the twisting polonaise, hiding as they were
behind the curtains in brocade
covered with hunting scenes,
seeing the parade of notes festive though death-dressed.
One day you discover from the ads
suspicious has the same look as discriminating,
that greeny tigers have hidden their skins on the leaves
of *Dieffenbachia*, ideas like onions are dropping their pale slips
to the floor, that the garden is a smile around the house,
and around what is hidden by the house.

Knowing What I Know Now

That Ruth means compassion

and ruthless is without and brutal as we expected

That each form broadens

and explains the original idea which can take forever

That nothing is complete

till all examples have been outlined and demonstrated

every leaf in Umfolozi

That first Jupiter is smothered by daylight only

to be the first in plain sight

while Mars is in Destin, Florida, hidden behind the Tastee Freez

That nothing's in isolation

but is accompanied by lists of relations

That what will be called miraculous

is inevitable and dross-common

If I think I have exceeded my limits they were not

If I say the two magnolias

in the yard are like paired lungs from which singing

is breath from the leaves

I am nowhere near what the normal will allow

GREY AREAS

Things are getting fuzzy when you see the words

aether, élan vital, fixed stars,

or hear someone say *No, that is impossible.*

It got no better when Mrs. Witherow

put four oranges and a flashlight on her desk

to explain the equinoxes

and then said they were seedless.

The world was swirling. How could that be so.

What about the miles of California,

what about the bees, the tiger perch

in Buck Lake spewing fry, what about the promise

I might see the light on the heavenly body

of someone I had not yet met.

What of the egg stories, anthers, pistils,

the sponge that was a plant, the plant that was an animal.

How much of this was lies just breaking us in

for the increasingly terrible to come.

THE SUN IN LEO

In the illustration a raj stands on the back of a lion that is a menagerie,

a sun grinning in his hand. Above in the light with no clouds

an astronaut's face shines off every instrument's window.

People and animals are moving in his legs as he spins against gravity.

In this sign real and impossible come together in tempera and Delrin

and someone down there is writing *My Life* before it's over

in another double bind of existence. People are trying to kill one other

and succeeding despite all these peaceful observations as Arabia slides by.

Blue and lonely oceans revolve. No getting around it, exotic's too common.

The explanation says Leo can be high-handed as well as high-minded

but everyone down here looking up is understandably nervous.

This is heaven and earth after all

where any story told about the other is an unlikely myth

and while we may not believe it we know our signs.

GHOST WRITER

Speech like smoke, air edgewise catching light

and denying like swerving birds,

like the baby's uncomprehending look

when recognized as the prophet reborn in the mountain village,

that drooler.

Now twice in three days I've seen silverfish.

One among my books, six dead and powdered under glass

and a mountainous image in a framed print

reborn as clouds and blended fog.

Now another night is added to the age of darkness, the same night

answering our wishes which are frivolous as golf.

When I think back, I realize since the noose was rediscovered,

everything's at risk.

MOON MISSING

I was so worried the hickory I recognized

had died from salt burn in the last hurricane

I may have passed by vervain and apple haw

like they didn't matter, but this spring

it put out seven shoots from its base.

Still, the oldest trick is the moon missing,

then the "new" moon appears,

though we know it's the old one, and we pretend

to be taken in like the mother or baby

behind the bath towel.

Really it's the moon winking,

being the stone that holds stones and now footprints.

And when I tell Frances, I see *she* is a moon

motionless in the doorway, skin reflecting

a lamp, a face that awakens on paper.

Out of the Whole Azalea

Out of the whole azalea, one branch quivers

and there is the lizard.

Blue jays scream rat snake for everyone

because tree bark moved.

I am watching for sand wasps hunting for females

when a leaf on its elbow

lies down, and a snake in the form

of a little river pours itself out from the litter.

It does not see me. Just as well. We are to be avoided.

We are listed in their books with the vicious.

They are merely poisonous to live.

Before the shot, anticipation, after it, the wasteful inequity.

Hunters are those for whom this is guiltless.

One slat irregular in the laddered blind, and there

the blazing eye of the neighbor.

Hours on End

Like baby corns in Cashew Chicken the ideas of the soul are plentiful
and poorly developed. Stacked end to end they would still reach nowhere.
Now Marvin who told us about the old days at Vanderbilt is gone
and his lawn chairs the salt air has eaten too thin to sit on are disappearing.
During his funeral an impossible feather was afloat in the birdless house.
I might have known once how this happened but I cannot see small as I used to.
Once I thought I saw the fur of life around a stone in the difficult river at St. Croix.
Later I had a microscope but the stone was gone and I imagined its surface
of algae meadows and caddisflies. I saw its long roots finally enter Louisiana.
In another of the tiny arts of recognition I say raise your hand everyone
who remembers oilcloth that stuck to your forearms or has discovered the ocean
whose wavelets only touch shore in our hearts, the long lonely here and now
in front of the viscous window behind which things wobble or vaguely pass by.

PURE INDONESIA

A pinwheel in the heart spins off oxygen like sparks
people singing anthems try to cover with their hands.
A pure Indonesia under my pillow opens its markets
every night to music, caged birds bought to be released
recalling the man who after winning the lottery tried
to buy out of business all the pet stores in Orlando.
Someone is writing up another confessional nightmare,
a universe made offhandedly by a young punk god
still working on his first, in which teeth and neon
play inordinate roles with willful murder. After all
who are we seeing most: those shooting husbands,
who owns the unbearable
and must pay and pay, ministers of slavemaking,
bodysnatching, those repaying through the nose.
In mine, nothing is concise. Cats are not required.
And no churchmen, only the college of red cardinals,
flames alight on Pyracantha, surviving cold & color,
where in no time, stars on my arm, I am in Jakarta.

Frequent Flyer

One does not tell the future   it tells us

when it arrives

People call and though I say wrong number

they call back

Last night I saw trampled grass where a deer

or refrigerator slept

and with light through lace like moon through leaves

during an eclipse

the whole room rested many times on your shoulder

It was like sitting on my leg

then rising up and feeling the stars pass through

each blood cell

You turned and glittered like a mirror ball

I have awakened

after working all night somewhere else

just to take aspirin for sore shoulders

and thought maybe someone lives here with my name

or the lines in my hands are maps

to my aching other life folded in a fist

since even the moon sometimes keeps its one eye closed

above the whole population

LOCAL NEWS

In the old days news stayed nearby
sometimes never leaving the scene of its origin
News that spread was meant to convince us for effect—
harrow making ribbons of the man in Kansas
who blasphemed machinery
how lightning touched a silcock and soured cows

How after a dove has spoken
the air is more tender in that place
The local news is motionless and dries
around the event leaving a hardly perceptible ring
Sometimes a marker will be placed near an incident
so readers must go to it
instead of leaving to wander the country mouth to mouth

Last night in the yard I passed Minneapolis
but it was only gardenias calling bees
no news at all but pleading
As a child I knew I was sleeping when I began
falling though still furled in my sheets
and I would look over other people's shoulders
to see what they were reading

The headlines the footnotes

EXTRA EXTRA

a boy has left his room through the map on the wall

There was an Era of Ashes

It has not passed

There was an Age of Labored Breathing

It has not passed

There were Centuries of Paradisiacal Waters

They are over

There was a Decade of Wax Hands

There was a Season of Too-Tight Strings

a Spring of Sharp Edges

a Week of Folding Birds out of Paper

a Day of Coin Silver

an Hour of Renaming Bones

There was a Minute of Not Here Not Now

Wait a second ...

We lived in these bodies from the beginning
even when daylight was getting up before we did
We lived together and apart and lived on salt water
on the short-grass plains, on nonstop talking

>

We lived on paper

>

We would wake up talking of another life
Within writing the same would happen
our eyes could be open, staring how the trees
scuffled up a hawk from raw materials

Our question was always what did you dream
when I wasn't with you

The bodies had nonstop dreams in them

Pictures of the body were not the body
but with them we could find our way

In one illustration the palm of a hand opened

to catch broadcasts of song   watercolored noises

laced with life directed to ossicles of the inner ear

shading the eyes cupping the auricle

listening as an illustration explained longing

how the earth was humming the sun vibrating

like a bell

>

The body was not a book though it had an appendix

and miracles and disasters   a beginning and an end

>

The unknowns sang down the sun   arpeggio arpeggio rest

The sadder the bodies the harder they whispered as they passed

>

We saw crows in the zodiac, roosters told the wind

We saw a plaid blanket asleep in the dog bed, dog or not

We saw obligations, the number of things dependent on us

including the overwhelming from which we were indistinguishable

>

We saw how a mind could make a world every minute

from little or no information, imagine past lives

a notion as bold as strangers entering a neighborhood

in broad daylight with a truck to carry off stereos

>

We imagined everything could be like a movie, a song

"Forever in Love" by The Four Swoons, cozy, a fireplace

and quilts in forest cabins, candles, tropical islands,

continuous singing, SAC bombers gassed in mid-air

for the illusion of security, forks to the left, face to the fire,

orgasms

We could explain things because we devised the system

Spaces within trees were figures the limbs drew deliberately

Wrinkles in time were a garment too big for us

We pushed back its sleeves to retard the season

and see another spring in Oregon

>

We could keep the day up all night with illuminations

with the words in our breaths that fogged windows equally

whether we said deathdread   wood thrush or diadem

The tide harvested water and the little starched moon

left over from last night couldn't even strangle a shadow

>

We could use yesterday's clouds all over again

the old light and glass and reflections of the leafy yard

We would watch for the edges of outside becoming inside

and the sign at Mike's Garden saying the ladybugs were in

PANTHEON

I was in a globe of air, an eye
with a floor that photographed heavens,
an eye I could walk into from a sunny plaza,
into rock created by water and lime rubble
when you touched me awake taking the remote.
I think soluble means the soul can dissolve
in two places at once as Michael makes a fish
or turkey appear in the third grade
from the same decorated pinecone.
Time for 20/20 you said, and stepping back
into the squinting difference of shadow and light,
I was back again, and saw love was the very thing
an earth must offer to keep its inhabitants, or lose.
I remembered again that dreaming is forgetting
and remembering at once and losing the difference,
why ocean creatures don't dissolve in their vast experience,
how birds, apparently flying down from a pale sky
or coffered ceiling, turn to leaves the instant they hit.

NEGOTIATING WITH DETAILS

I don't know anyone you know. I merely leaned over
the dock to handwash when the bottom up and shuddered.
A stingray large as a card table resting in my depth of field
floated off, its edges rippling, and I refocused to understand.
These things happen to remind us of the great community
where no one knows anyone. But through such revelations
is reunion, and implications of parallel things lost in hearing
despite the beautiful ampersands and treble clefs on either side
of our heads, the low hum of bacteria, flagellates dividing
like tape unsticking, imagining music is just background
till that one song and you drop everything to listen. The words,
partly obscured by a child's milk moustache, a blanket moving
back and forth over their sleeping bodies not by their doing.
Maybe you're just anxious. That x implied in the middle
of words like *crossroads, crosshairs*. There there.
A *shhh* of assurance like the x spoken in the overwhelming
sound-scale vibration of ocean and Xochimilco.

EVERYTHING FOLLOWING

The weathering of wood, that is beautiful,

fraying, beautiful.

The blond hair caught in the bandage,

that also, for itself.

The becoming and ruins that intrigue us.

Everything actual

and their exceptional referents,

nothing out of context.

A hand selecting a marble from a glass bowl,

limbs cluttered by daylight,

soot at night.

Maybe the tub feet are memories

of a great hawk grasping the globe it feeds on

or the squirrel stuffing acorns in crevices

as today along the sea wall,

and the flicker coming after, removing them.

Maybe it was not a great hawk,

but a great woodpecker, or an average woodpecker

and a great acorn, everything following

something else with beautiful intentions.

Nothing is ordinary.

Day and night being the same dream

from which we never awaken, never actually sleep.

PANORAMA

A rented room on a semi-famous hill, where years ago a balcony

with three sides and French floor-to-ceiling windows opened inward

under a cathedral ceiling in Rome and someone said Guarda la veduta.

When Lovell said the earth fit behind his thumb more people

discovered themselves, though they had been covering the moon

on their own for years, and the sun too for convenience.

But they were out there, alone as mental illness, looking back.

From there, we could see everything but St. Peter's and the round chapel

behind the American Academy where a monk, an ecclesiastical outpatient

given this jurisdiction, would speak to visitors

in eight languages while showing the chapel you had to climb down to,

collecting their change. He mentioned frescos, and the light,

and Bosch's other Magus, what's-her-name, Adam's other wife,

Sophia, antimatter, wind chimes he could hear through bicycle bells,

and the life we sleep away, the body we use for it, the whole world

stretching out before our beds.

DOWN IN THE DISTANCE

I am trying to go small and listen to the cells
synthesizing my glittering belongings
and acknowledge the red words in the text:
hemoglobin, oxygen, radium from pitchblende.
We do not need dynamos and heavy equipment.
Look what is accomplished by just the moderate heat
of a body. We can see farther than we hear,
love longer than we last. Our engines are monuments
to how we are missing the boat, even though the boat
is a sidetrack like mixing our metaphors that sink.
Down in the distance, the enzymes catalyze glucose
to pyruvate, little snaps like cracking your knuckles.
My right hand reaches for yours. Blood parses water.
I am relying on minute uncertainties. I am answering
the atmosphere as if it spoke like voices from oxidation,
infection, a burning bush.

Nightmare

Memory comes with its own gauze curtains and hazy furniture.

It's a wonder we can lounge on them at all.

Figures undressing behind screens, animals passing room to room,

scenes inconsistent. They flash informally for miles,

and miles in reverie are like inches on a map.

You can be anywhere in no time, only your leg has fallen over

on your wife, your arms not traveling at all.

Even this solidity is not enough since impossible things are common.

The chirps of door locks are swallows bloody with sunset.

In the downpour, vans are spinning off I-10 like electrons.

Kate radios them in. Turkeys leave the trees on impact,

dispersing like epithets. Comfortable assumptions

are collapsed and stacked in the corner with the folding chair.

BIRD HOUSES BY MAIL

Still

houses are no guarantee. Of course I knew
I could have made my own but like the spider
that built a web between the lock and its tumblers
so it operated without danger—there are experts.
Look at this house. With the doors of each room
open or closed I imagine circulation like a heart.
I cannot name the insects that try to pass through
the windows but none are so astounding in their travel
as when Gordon Allen the only science teacher
in art school cranked his machine and sent lightning
through Flo Sheldon's notebook. For an instant
the invisible went solid. The bluebirds were fewer
even then. They moved as the cool reminded.
They rose in little clouds like bubbles in water
about to be ice. Nothing could keep them any more
than electrons be prevented from leaving the brass ball.
The flyer says they may not come the first year.
Or ever really. Maybe never at all.

HEADLINES

Cumulus scrubs out blue like I clean windows with dry newspapers.

Headlines reaffirm we learn geography by wars. Dark matter supposedly

takes up most of what we think is nothing. I know I am completely

transparent to the fly unless I move and I know black is not nothing

any more than white is fire on the stars. As for the others

I know are with me I would catch them if I could twist fast enough.

The ones behind me I see just far enough to know their shadows.

Now this is news. The past. The other sun behind our own we never see.

Brian we picked up hitching who saw auras as fields around us

and I saw them too but mostly through the window   how they knitted

across the valleys like afghans. Ours striped yellow. I know well enough

the printed word picks up things heartsick and oily like a litho. I don't

believe everything I read. I know they poignantly linger though cleaned

the way dead-for-months-dog odor rises from the carpet with shampoo.

EVOLUTION

So our toes and fingers were all roots, once touching,
and a body sometimes grown up
to a standing beast that later came loose from the earth,
nails painted red.
The tips of our backbones grew from their processes,
sunbursts, and then receded.
The hair on our bodies had been spines like a cactus,
had been grass growing
like water in the wind, and peach fur before that flowered
in the light
like the painted paper-thin azaleas bolted to the walls
of the St. Charles Inn
that opened with dawn and closed like breathing.

Still, I thought to escape from my birth family
like rockets the earth.
The lesson of change is there are no isolated cases,
and it's not an error because things don't go as we'd planned,
nor an accident when they do.
Such things are often decided in the last minute
like lightning's stepped leader,
down from clouds, finding the least resistance every few hundred yards
until the discharge rises to meet it.

Only real life has slower zig-zags, leaving its burn marks on us,

foolprints one can follow,

made not with our feet, but presumptions

that everyone is satisfied

and will cheer wildly

if their hometown is mentioned.

FAMOUS CANARIES

Once when half the San Carlos was demolished we saw things
sprayed on the walls about someone named Chico we never suspected.
Then Liz called. She'd met a Brazilian and her headaches went away.
Perhaps she was nervous after her father and then one brother
with no warning collapsed leaving the shower. As if what happened
underground was suddenly visible the dust was so thick
from destruction I thought of past miners and their waltzing mice
so active in their wire cages any slowdown was serious. As hard to think
a man might take an animal into the earth to be his next-to-last-breath
as thinking she would leave for Arizona with another name as protection.
Her x husband still looks down on the Bay and its regular breathing
the way she remembered twice a year goldfinches sulphured the air
to and from Manitoba. Glittered like dust. Or the soft and predictable
coal-colored fish crows that loaded and unloaded trees below their window.
Both directions have their risks. When they broke through to the miners
in Wheeling they'd left notes for their loved ones as the wall above Garden Street
made those boasts for someone as a predictor of some wild promise in the dark.
Now he is coming up for air. His legs are moving. Must be dreaming on his wheel.
She is closing her eyes in her yellow nightgown. Not a peep out of her.
Just retelling the simplest fact is drama. So far nothing has exploded.

There were echoes speaking to emptiness

There were voices saying something in Hawaiian

whose vowels rushed over each other like water on new lava

There were handwritten letters of enormous power

There were names that floated like scarves above shrubbery

There were numismatists and philatelists

and multiple personalities of light

There were flags snapping like crisp footsteps

There were trees whose leaves were identical adjectives

There were certain words unavailable on Sundays

things so compelling illustration was unnecessary

There were serious times when appropriate dress was latex

gloves and paper shoes There were heartbreaks like glass

There were stark reminders

Let's say it took acres to confirm the lights were moving
away from us, though one was Freeman's kitchen window
and the Red Shift, like the rate of inflammation, was Howard's
bloodshot eyes from another night of bourbon longing for his wife.

Let's say there was the world and mirrors that made things closer,
miles of fence and the four lights connecting pasture to the stars
and interstates, acres of miles of longing and remorse.

>

We could see how many pot shots had missed the moon,
heard how many frogs made the sound of water for the lake

We saw the sign of cupped hands, the hearth stones,
the three-starred belt, the sword of Orion containing a galaxy.

>

Nothing explained the widening dark

>

Let's say the wet sky early was alizarin and loving
merely opening its echoing dark eyes, rivers,
rivers saying their secret non-consonantal names,
big long liquid ones that gargled, and equally
the rivulets echoed smaller from their cranny floods

Let's say we could not make maps fast enough.
The genders came and went. This for a minute,
that and back like the Mississippi that spills its banks
then retrieves them, all the big redfish, males.

>

Let's say we were blood cells in a larger being, or the planet was,
and we were the platelets and fractions.
Or we inhabited bubbles in a boil of all the brocade angels of the Orient,
while at night we heard insects open their packages,
a vast star crackle unwrapping around us.

>

Let's say it might have been only a moment of high sodium
that separated songs on the radio from the whole house
as off in the distance cities could be seen swaying,

>

and it took only a slight constriction of iris to separate the gar
from leaf shadow at Clyde and Niki's paradise in paradise
in the orchid and grass-dense glass-slick Everglades

Let's say it was like being in a maze of neurons like a brain
where nature was richly thinking to itself.

>

Let's say we could imagine life in a small blue flame
even in December and turn, when frazzled,
not to the medicine cabinet but to the window,
the backyard, the healing garden, the articulate swamp.

>

Let's say it was as if the night lights we tried to remember, blurred,
shimmying as heat, compelling but unclear,
as if solid form loosened a shadow given light almost glasslike
like the shadow of dreams in daylight that lingered
like smoke on our clothes

like the huge informality of fire, the dreamy colors
firemen recall falling before trees,
carried off still warm on their yellow, buckled slickers.

>

Let's say the body of your body appeared in daylight
to see if the shoes fit and you were the ghost you heard about
with your toes glowing, the door-to-door spirit of October
wearing inside out bones, the werewolf awakening in human form
on a riverbank spotted with blood, and under you footprints
and the names of the angels of podiatry: Talus   Phalanges.

Let's say we made up stories from profound misunderstanding,
one of which was the necessity of guilt, a product like a dress shoe
you would grow into though it blistered and never fit.
Its failure was supposed to be your fault and you paid with your life.

Still, don't think we hadn't noticed the wheels on the furniture
that could roll away at any moment as if a stage set,
how the carved chairs with wings and garlands were prepared
to fly off from the living room scattering flowers,

and what were their shapes anyway but straw fill and wires,

how could one wake up right in the middle of one's body

and be lost even when the bedclothes filled in

and furniture occupied again its convenient pretenses.

>

Let's say it might have been only humidity, the clouds

all racing and erasing, the shaky longhand of birds

coming and going, even the oceans never decided.

Let's say how often we woke just as daylight was opening

its complicated watch, the chickadees *tsk*ing

long minutes from the oaks, one dream having let go

at the last minute its daylight-saving heartbeats

on which the doctor eavesdropped with a rubber hose.

Needless

Four birds carved in Thailand with skill that can miss a few feathers,

be painted differently each time, and still be truthful.

Imagination is creating the possible, its best work.

Gaudy-winged frogs, four-legged whistlebirds whose horns curve back

to be handles are strange only till they find one in Surinam

and feature its habits on Discovery.

That little stick-sound we know is bare feet in slippers,

that little blur of mouse scratching its cheek with a hind paw,

the wasp seeing pathways into the violet light, swatter arcing to the fly

feeling the railing with its mouth like a blind lover,

the yellow dots, black, magenta, cyan, hovering together like a vertigo.

But today a Spanish Dancer nudibranch and angels appeared in the newspaper,

thousands in plastic bags taken wholesale from rivers of the world.

Stop. There is no need to spread the animals everywhere.

No reason everyone should have a collection including a few of everything.

That is what the mind is for.

No Wonder

Many think life
is like people singing in a language they failed in high school,
breaking spontaneously into dance
while outside
a few of the downed leaves pick up
and run in a parody of animals.
Afternoon will be full
of these transformations.
Some of wind. Some light. Some because strings
of the doily spider connect to everything.

A thumb and forefinger touching is OK.
An opportunity wren-sized whose cozy architecture
is everything waiting on the other side.
The orgiastic insect-laden hum of hearts.
July.
The time when a sudden flush has shrew-leaves
and otter-children spinning in an eddy on the deck
and you feel you might actually honk
this time if you love something,
if you regret something
you can't take back or talk about.
But just because

some ivory gulls are passing for nurses
with giveaway feet and the wall mirror is a kind of upright bed
and all of the laundry behind us is visible
and refuses to fold down
changes nothing, or just because it lets go its images
to remind us to be neat, to stay combed,
in short to be an organ like liver, or the skin containing
the sheet music held up to be read.
It's no wonder one could be confused
whether the quavers were music or fear.

LOST AND FOUND

What can really be predicted,
and what is good as guessed at,
is like looking into the freezer to learn about the Arctic caribou
wearing their bunny slippers down from the Brooks Range.
Finding the right place
is hard as marrying a river with a gold ring.

Say you are getting to know someone and they turn sideways
and suddenly there's a hidden twin,
or you see her on TV, the weather woman in a tailored suit
one cheek still wrinkled from a dream,
and you could have been either in another life.
Such alternatives happen
just as it's possible to take a wrong turn   miss your real parents
and wind up in Iowa instead.

Much in the Lost and Found stays lost.

An east wind sends shadows on the ruffled surface
flicking like the dock on fire.
It looks the same as hair braiding with glass from a sunset window.
Look what the body has,
and has more of the longer you look, maybe everything you need.

Not just any body,
but the one that like last spring left a mark
as if sleeping on your cheek all winter.
This mistake is mercy at its best.

Here at the Intersection

A mute TV is just another window deprived of dialog.
The figures seem curiously insane. A man speaks to graduation
from the stage with such electric distortion no one can understand
anything behind him and yet everyone proceeds as if all is normal.
They listen and line up for their incomprehensible diplomas.
Between the blood meal and recognition are the sauces and forks
the left-handed napkin and the 3-spooned heraldry of metals.
Culture is putting more equipment and ritual between us
and what we are actually doing. By the time we are fully civilized
we will have obscured the origins of everything. Here at the intersection
are small white crosses. After the hurricane the scrawled names
of insurance companies appeared on the leftover walls. Scrolled names.
The figures seem curiously insane. You cannot see a thing long enough
to understand. Mr. Lincoln pulled back the curtains on the French doors
and left the White House on three occasions to have his son dug up
just to look again upon his face.

FACTS OF LIFE

In the whole sky twirling

this minute there is only one cloud shaped like Sri Lanka.

Its red collar of topsoil

seen from space is a dampening bandage.

Eleven white ibis mistaken for clouds are too worried to stop

lest someone have a gun or lack of understanding

along the perfectly visible local coast.

And of course they do, and a landscape with saws

—sunset—sunset,

the cut and rake teeth hidden in the words.

Clouds change easily,

birds pass unrecognized, but mystery for us

is uncommon little giveaways:

sunset at Half Moon, someone in a tux on Haight Street,

potters in Cairo, swimmers from Alcatraz

in another trick of expectation.

Outside my window a windsock became a mast.

A flame with its ragged ends

on a rowboat far behind it as if on fire.

As we looked it came down to us.

It flew. It heeded. It heeled.

HITTING THE HOT SPOTS

Carol who would not hurt the fruit flies heat-stunned
on the red bedspread under her goose-neck reading lamp
slipped paper we still call typewriter under two and moved
them closer to the phone hoping they'd recover.
She imagined how things small as punkies or dixie midges
are picked up in storms or tornadoes and live a whole life moving
from the first fingering updraft in Texarkana through the dust-
fisted dynamo sidewinder ending the other side of the trailer
park in Mission, Kansas—that standing in the stereo half-acre
of Vivaldi cranked to nine is a kind of pressured equivalent
to an afternoon alone in Denali's live silence or Biscayne afloat
above coral with a snorkel a larva turning slowly as one
of the Gulf Stream's glassy animals Jeffersonian and Emersonian
at once and closer to the sun. When she whirled and slapped
a mosquito and missed a red hand stayed on her leg throughout
most of the chapter on Self-Reliance.

THE COMMON INSISTS

In spite of the overwhelming reliability of things,

the wind making rivulets on my sleeve same as window glass,

the same rocks shaped by the same reasons on Mars.

I am like a cricket singing to another sore voice. I hear it,

but faithful to symmetry, I don't move closer.

It may not be singing to me. Movement may lead to dissolution.

Stars could make up new animals. The dragonfly

might chase the swallow as it did today in warning.

I am living at the edge of light looking out

over water that touches Mexico. The edge of the continent

holds hands with inlets and I mention them over and over

as if no one listened last time. The common insists.

Lynx and orchids for some. Underwinter life below the ice.

From here I wave to you like polishing the air.

ARTIFICIAL LIGHT

As if the houses went berserk and lacked bones
like the list of dead acquaintances
and the breakfront and spindlework recalled the animals:
cattle   deer   bison
on their dainty legs
staircases that gathered in the glow of dusk
dreading the winter   pleading by presence
realizing the city longed for the fields
forest for clearings where a village might be seen
beyond a stretch of clover
a child at a window with a cat

Pure amateurs preferred a long exposure to magnesium
ignited by a spark
Either way it seemed so far from normal
to actually look at one's ancestors
Then after a year of silence on the very day
I put a letter in the mail to Willy in Colorado
he called and both theoretical houses
smiled from their moorings
softened their mutual porches towards collapse
We should have known once we had seen
through Madam Roentgen's hand still with its ring
what could be hidden   what could stop us

Modern Communication

Do I have to think of everything she said in the letter. Of course.
And remember luck is deep in the bones the nickname for dice
referring to a world so small and b/w we think we can rely on it.
Everything's manageable and seen from the twelve small windows
looking out on diminishment presumed to be fun.
In the tropics they bring you ice crystals flavored with mint
because it's difficult. Wealth mingles the opposites. Now there's that song
about the limitation of numbers. Nature's so concerned
with keeping to itself it's like a bird in your presence singing
in the voice you recognize but out of sight becoming a hyena harlequin
an operatic thrush with a nose ring and long blue ankles.
Wind fills a spinnaker as if a brain had opened momentarily
over the water, something permanent in the pilot whale. A sign
that a huge natural intelligence has gathered in that place
becoming visible where we thought nothing existed but light air.
You hear thumps in the earth. Eglin. Blood drum and sunburn.
The landscape sets fire to itself at sundown or an arsonist on Garcon Point.
Then your shadow akin to flooding enlarges to cover everything.
On a moonless night you enact what becomes modern communion.
The laptop opens the green/grey light of the more contemporary moon
and the recent future of remembering begins.

GHOST STORY

We know the occupants. They tell us a true ghost
in this world is lost, and any living in your house
should be counseled out. But those of the everyday,
the spook glimpsed in the coffee pot, the book
opening its pages to what you were thinking
by itself, the leaf shadows becoming rats on the lawn
of the Rhode Island Historical Society, pets switching
from one life to another after an owner's exit, or reverse,
are this world's, and cherished, just as the apples are not
dead but seem so, falling and rotting and suffering wasps
in their abdomens striped with night and a sunny day,
and carry the idea, or promise of life in death, the way
we might replace words with an almost natural equivalent,
permission for persimmon, for instance.

PLENTY FOR US

One gull touches down
A moth takes its place, rising like a second thought
Reality is both created and displayed
Shore breaks, on breaking
become amphipods and crabs,
scattering to sawgrass
in the take-back and give
like the pass-it-on notes in school

Little can resist this touch-and-go,
this plenty-for-us,
but the gods have never been happy
We have not been asking about them often enough
so they are always coming to earth, butting in,
to see if their pictures are still on the mantle,
their carvings stuck in the archways
Did we save their threatening letters,
their lies about life,
and might the cameras we designed to touch light into memory
alter their descent, prolong them

We put up with gravity

We worshipped those beautiful among us

We had books of angels They were in them

We missed the marvelous staring us in the face daily

Misspelled the marvelous from disbelief in spelling

We tried to make permanence out of shoddy materials

We unmade permanence by disavowing history

We said there were nine planets

We took one back for not being big enough

We rethought the decision

We felt partial to buffalo grass

We named places for things no longer there

We brought out the worst

We refused in spite of evidence

We spoke too soon

We said bloodstream as if a sun rose above it,

swallows on its banks, eddies, and a life inside.

We were this and what occurred to us because of it

and could be dammed and have current and knives inside,

a sagging farmhouse downstream, a purpose

we went numb before, even the dusting snow on hillsides

were leucocytes, skin cells. We were waterproof, but burned.

>

We found pictures bolted to the walls as if we were so desperate

for images we might even steal prints of top-hatted English

arriving for foxes with their paper dogs, buds on the ash,

finches turning gold at the feeders, egg white frames,

seasons so neat symmetry was medicine.

Understanding was there but stopped short of us,

like mail unopened, a song empty of words,

a dance whose opponent was gravity, fallen leaves that blacken.

>

There were lights everywhere   The body was not dark

even slight pressure on the eyes showed a bijoux

the surgery channel had us multicolored as a reef

our viscera displayed like a wreck of Christmas

There were bird-chested people, angels with sterna

where the wing muscles would attach

There were house finches hovering to break the beam

and open the doors to the seed-filled Garden Shop

>

There were lines in our hands mysterious as game trails

lines waiting patiently for explanations of longing

Tongue standing for the whole language   mother tongue

even for the dead buried with scripts in their mouths

just in case the stories were true and we showed up

speechless before a globular cluster

>

There were times we thought the ocean was the silent world

despite miles of snow quenched by touch, exchanges of oxygen and temperature, despite a trillion trillion clattering glass hands.

There were times we could hardly hear anything

over the sound of a day breaking

There were times cathedrals went up in shadows

and a catwalk was traveled by figures, by cats,

whose substance was voices discussing last night,

how many times red and green lights changed places

how we moved and some of the loose stars moved

>

There were times when the dark was our nerves—

maybe a phone going off, an urgent knock

demanding an answer, a clock, a mad buzzer,

a friend drunk leaning on the bell.

There were times when anxiety was justified,

one bubble could kill us after all,

times when a dream was so dry even a thick tongue

could taste it, the acid hint of lime before alcohol.

>

There were times glass would cry out itself,

even unbroken, little shrieks from rubbing

with water and ammonia while trying

to make the yard and dining room come closer

and times we did ourselves, unable to save thrushes

and warblers, believers in a deep and continuous world

stacked against the windows

>

There were days and days layered above us interspersed with storms,

the rubble of night's black stones, slums in the mind as well as Chicago

There were lemurs that never knew Sri Lanka

There were only our bodies

Time was cows chewing the same fields over and over

There were times when complete fabrications were true,

when an entire life existed between speech and disbelief,

a nanosecond sunrise, then rain and disaster, fictional moments lengthened,

denials gone soft, some remaining false despite suggestions

that the moon was a manhole in the lake

>

There were times the sky we lived in was so dense
we hardly moved through its substance,
times when nothing we thought we knew was true
and we were connected by nothing we could prove

>

There were times we thought we could tell how many
dreams to an ounce, drams to a fathom,
how vetch twirled like dervishes, why things rioted around us,
why we pulled language up over our heads while below
we kicked off the covers

>

There were times when there was no having the last word
and the secret names were gibberish

There was no common there was again differently

Acknowledgments

Many thanks to the editors of the following publications in which these poems first appeared, sometimes under other titles and in earlier versions: *Another Chicago Magazine*, *Bayou*, the *Believer*, *blastie*, *Boston Review*, *Buckle &*, *Cloudbank*, *Curious Rooms*, *ForPoetry.com*, *Full Circle*, *Verse Daily*, *Gettysburg Review*, *Indiana Review*, *Innisfree*, *Kestrel*, *Laurel Review*, *Lullwater Review*, *Marlboro Review*, *Maryland Poetry Review*, *Other Voices International*, *Prick of the Spindle*, *Panhandler*, the *Salt River Review*, the *Southeast Review*, *Stray Dog*, *storySouth*, *Typo*, the *2 River View*.

I am honored to have been chosen to be part of the new McSweeney's Poetry Series, and I am especially indebted to Jesse Nathan and Dominic Luxford for that selection, and for their inspired collaborative vision, which brought this volume to completion. Thanks also to the staff at McSweeney's whose participation in design, copy editing, fact checking, and attention to details were so important in the book's production.

My very special thanks also goes to poet and critic Stephen Burt, who has been a supporter of my work from the first book. And of course, to my wife Frances Dunham, who has lived through these poems with me and is such a part of them.

I'd like to thank the bird that was not one
but a reflection from the glass door opening outward
then nesting on the bookcase,
the many snails at night whose glistening paths
showed me that apparently random is purpose
without a backbone.
My thanks to the house cracking its knuckles
and to blocks of historic old roses in Foley
named for archdukes and queens,
to house wrens singing as if on a burning floor
ladders couldn't reach.
Special recognition goes to the tug Kaitlin Oliva
for pushing against a vast fugitive blue
and for its painted name I read without glasses,
old radios tuning in stars between stations.
I want to acknowledge the influence of things
expanding and compressing at different rates,
people throwing money into even a dry sluice
in sheer expectation that water will hear them,
the streamers of wisteria, the philosophies
of duration and expectation without which
I might never have so cheerfully persisted.
I note my debt to the billowing flights of pine whites,
jellyfish ascending with a pulsing motion
that soothed me, being such a pushover for love
I want to mention my gratefulness for the hours
when I was encouraged by bioluminescence,
by immanence, intrinsic musics, the marvelous
chaotics of weather and suggestible affections
and especially how I never could have done this
without everything I've left out, and fragrance
and what distance does to color.

About the Author

Allan Peterson has been awarded fellowships from the National Endowment for the Arts and the state of Florida. His poems have appeared in the *Nation*, *Boston Review*, *Agni*, the *Paris Review*, the *Believer* and dozens of other magazines, as well as several anthologies. Peterson's collection *Anonymous Or* won the Defined Providence Press competition in 2001, and his follow-up volume, *All the Lavish in Common*, won the 2005 Juniper Prize from the University of Massachusetts. Salmon Press (Ireland) published his most recent book, *As Much As*. He has a BFA in painting from the Rhode Island School of Design, an MFA in drawing from Southern Illinois University, was chair of the art department at Pensacola State College until his retirement in 2005, and currently divides his time between Gulf Breeze, Florida, and Ashland, Oregon.